Bri...
Travel Guide

Sightseeing, Hotel, Restaurant & Shopping Highlights

Sara Laing

Copyright © 2015, Astute Press
All Rights Reserved.

No part of this publication may be reproduced, stored in a retrieval system, or transmitted, in any form or by any means without the prior written permission of the publisher, nor be otherwise circulated in any form of binding or cover other than that in which it is published and without similar condition being imposed on the subsequent purchaser.

If there are any errors or omissions in copyright acknowledgements the publisher will be pleased to insert the appropriate acknowledgement in any subsequent printing of this publication.

Although we have taken all reasonable care in researching this book we make no warranty about the accuracy or completeness of its content and disclaim all liability arising from its use

Table of Contents

Brno 5
- **Culture** 8
- **Location & Orientation** 9
- **Climate & When to Visit** 11

Sightseeing Highlights 13
- **Freedom Square** 13
- **Spielberg Castle (Hrad Spilberk)** 15
- **Brno Zoo** 16
- **Roznov pod Radhostem (Mill Valley Open Air Museum)** 17
- **Cathedral of St. Peter & Paul** 18
- **Villa Tugendhat** 20
- **Capuchin Crypt & Church** 21
- **Moravian Karst, Caves & Cable Car** 22
- **Brno Labyrinth** 23
- **Moravian Art Gallery** 24

Recommendations for the Budget Traveller 27
- **Places to Stay** 27
  - Hostel Jacob 27
  - Hostel Fléda 28
  - Palacky Hotel & Hostel 29
  - Hostel Mitte 30
  - Ruta 80 31
- **Places to Eat & Drink** 32
  - Café Podnebi 32
  - Vyhlídka Sound Café Bar 33
  - Restaurant Varna 34
  - Kupe 35
  - Pivovarska Starobrno Brewery Restaurant 36
- **Places to Shop** 37
  - Olympia Brno 37
  - Luta 38
  - Cabbage Market (Zelny trh) 39
  - Masarykova Street 39
  - Bohemia Crystal 40

Brno

The second Czech Republic city of Brno is an interesting and less-visited alternative to the capital city, Prague. A number of major sights in Brno and the Moravian region are classified as national cultural sights in the Czech Republic. With nearly 400,000 people, Brno is located in the centre of Europe and is within 200 kilometres of both Prague and Vienna.

Brno was founded one thousand years ago and for many centuries it was the capital of Moravia. It is a city of varying architectural styles with many buildings dating from the boom times of the flourishing 19th century. As is quite common in Eastern Europe there are many beautiful palaces and castles.

The Old Town Hall with its ornate Gothic Gate is the oldest secular building in the city and an interesting feature is the slightly lopsided tower. The stonemason working on the construction was refused payment by the council so he deliberately left the tower crooked.

For a bit of fun join the locals and visitors alike at the bullet-shaped clock in Freedom Square. This modern clock has glass balls inside and on the hour of 11am they drop from top to bottom. Various holes in the sides mean that you can stick your hands and try to be the lucky one to catch one of the four marble sized balls. If you are successful you can keep it.

Don't however rely on looking at the black granite clock to tell you the time. Although it is possible to calculate the time from the rather complicated instructions it is easier to look at your watch.

The city is known for its heritage and folklore and many Czech Crowns are spent every year on cultural events. There are plenty of galleries, museums, palaces and castles to visit and after Prague the city is home to the largest historic preservation zone in the country.

A short ride from the city centre at Brno-Líšeň visitors can find waterfalls cascading down into the lakes of the Marian Valley surrounded by wooded hills while at Brno-Židenice the largish Jewish cemetery in Moravia can be visited. Along with the 12,000 or so elaborate family tombs, headstones and grave markers the Memorial to the Victims of the Holocaust from 1950 can be found behind the Romanesque Revival house of mourning at the entrance to the cemetery.

Even if you can't read the menu trying Czech cuisine is a must. Many restaurants offer a set lunchtime meal deal which makes it easier if your knowledge of the Czech language isn't quite up to scratch!

The traditional dishes are hearty and filling, with fried cheese and chips or roast pork, cabbage and dumplings being very popular. The dumplings are called halušky and the national dish of Slovakia is bryndzové halušky; dumplings topped with a sheep's cheese.

To drink there is the Czech beers of Starobrno, Urquel or Gambrinos and the intriguingly named "blood of Moravia" is the local high quality wine. For lovers of a certain dark and fizzy drink there is the local alternative of Kofola. Similar to its famous counterpart the taste is of liquorice but it is captivating and unmistakable.

If you look at the Czech language it would seem that someone stole most of the vowels! The dialect spoken in Brno is called Hantec and the roots can be traced back to the Second World War. It is a mixture of Czech, Yiddish and German. The dialect is not widely spoken but can be found in the city when it is used to confuse not only tourists but Czechs from other parts of the country. If you get stuck there are two tourist information centres in the town, Nádražní Street and Radnická Street.

Culture

Theatre lovers have several choices of where to go in Brno. The Brno City Theatre tends to have original works plus musicals and drama shows. At the bigger National Theatre there are three stages: Janáček Theatre, Reduta Theatre and the Mahen Theatre where a variety of performances can be seen. The Mahen Theatre has the honour of being the first theatre in Europe to be lit up by electric light bulbs.

For night owls there are several clubs in the city centre all within a 15 minute walk from each other including Two Faces, Metro and Remix. For a more soothing musical experience try Bar U Palečka for chamber music or some upbeat jazz music.

Brno is a well-known city in Central Europe for its annual trade fairs and events and around 40 such events are held there every year. The Brno Exhibition Centre has to be one of the prettiest sites for major events that you would find anywhere. Located in the green Pisárky valley the site was created in 1928 and the 16 pavilions and tree-lined walkways blend beautifully into the countryside.

The major engineering fair INVEX and the electronics fair DIGITEX both draw thousands of visitors to this elegant site while others include Autosalon Brno, an international motor show and the Pivex beer fair and Vinex wine fair.

Another huge event held annually in Brno is the Moto GP when 200,000 fans descend on the Masaryk Circuit for the thrill and speed of the world's biggest motorcycling championship.

For noise of a different kind with plenty of added colour and excitement the Ignis Brunensis is an annual event that lights up the skies. The biggest draw is the Fireworks Competition which creates an amazing atmosphere and draws in big crowds.

Ignis Brunensis is held in the Denis Gardens and kicks off the start of the summer tourist season in Brno and lasts for a whole month from the last week of May each year. There is also the Balloon Jam where dozens of hot air balloons make splashes of colour in the Brno sky, Conjuror's Night, Museum Night, Transport Nostalgia and the Dragon Boat Race as well as loads of other fun and festivities.

Location & Orientation

From a geographical point of view Brno is situated in an excellent position. Midway between the capitals of the Czech Republic and Austria, Prague and Vienna, it makes adding any or all of them on to your itinerary easy. The city is the cultural and administrative centre of the South Moravian Region and lies in a basin of the Svitava and Svratva rivers and on three sides there are thickly forested hills.

The population of city area is around 400,000 with around 90,000 of people being students from both home and abroad who come to study in the 12 universities in this beautiful area of the Czech Republic.

Brno-Tuřany Airport is only a few miles from the centre. The airport is small and fairly basic but has everything necessary as regards shops, car hire and money exchange. There is a bus between the city and airport every 15 minutes.

There are actually more flights to nearby Prague and Vienna so sometimes this is the easier option and then catch a bus from these cities to Brno.

To get around in Brno there is an Integrated Transport System which encompasses the buses, trams and trolleybuses. It is called Salina and you buy the ticket according to the zone and length of journey. Tickets can be bought from kiosks and tobacconists as well as the yellow ticket machines at the tram stops. For travelling further afield there is a half hourly bus service to Prague.

Brno is an important stop on the train line that stretches from the Balkan Peninsula through to Scandinavia and all Eurocity trains stop at the station. The train station is conveniently located a short walk from the city centre.

A quieter way to travel and enjoy the scenery is on the electric powered boats out on the Brno Reservoir. Between April and October there are a number of boats that take visitors on peaceful tours round the water. The quayside at Bystrc is easy to reach by ubs from the town centre.

Climate & When to Visit

Brno is a great place all year round as it has reasonable summers and chilly winters but never suffers from any extremes of weather. The air quality is excellent as the air circulates naturally when compared to other Czech cities.

As winter turns into spring the lowest temperature is around 0°C but as summer approaches the mercury rises to 19.5°C making it a great time for walks in the Lužánky park, sightseeing around the city and going up to Spielberg Castle. In early spring coats and jumpers will still be needed but on the warmer days lighter clothes can come out of the wardrobe.

In the height of summer temperatures of 25°C can be reached with occasional bursts of much warmer weather. Brno in summer is super place with lots of outdoor space, beautiful forests and hills to enjoy and rivers and lakes to cool off in. The parks are full of couples walking hand-in-hand, families enjoying picnics under the shady trees and shorts and t-shirts are all that are needed. The summertime low of 11°C in the evenings means you might need to take a light wrap or jacket out with you. The end of June is prone to thunderstorms so be prepared!

With lots of trees providing colour as autumn comes Brno is a pretty place to visit. The weather is still warm enough for shirt sleeves in the early part of the season with temperatures of 20°C.

However, the change in weather can be quite rapid and as the winter months get closer the nighttime low of just 1°C will have you reaching for thicker duvets, socks and warm jumpers.

Winter is fairly average with a high of around 3°C and a low of -5°C in January but most living accommodation has central heating and carpets so being indoors is usually ok. Outside wear sensible shoes or boots and wrap up warmly and drink medovina. Snow does fall in Brno but being light to moderate it isn't too much of a problem. The snow tends to be deepest around mid-January with an average depth of around four inches.

Sightseeing Highlights

Freedom Square

Follow the signs for Namesti Svobody and you will arrive in Freedom Square, a wide-open and pleasant square that is mainly traffic free, just look out for the tram. It is a super place to stroll round and then sit at a pavement café and watch the world go by. Originally known as Lower Market it is on a level with some of the most famous squares in the world such as Times Square, Trafalgar Square and Tiananmen Square.

In the square are the grumpy, clumsy men statues known as Mamlas that adorn an elegant building towards the southern end. The rather odd shaped bullet clock is close to the Mamlas and there is also the Parnassus Fountain which is the finest piece of sculpture in Brno. It was designed in the 1690's by Fischer von Erlach and is a very theatrical piece full of trompe-l'oeil and Baroque design.

In the Northwest Corner the baroque style Plague Column 1679 dominates the square and this is in memory of victims of the plague. Near the centre of the square if you look carefully you can still see the remains of the Church of St. Nicholas that stood in the square for centuries. Much of the square was built in the 13th century and now a mixture of old and new buildings stand side by side filled with shops, bars and restaurants. Schwarz Palace is now a modern shopping gallery but the entrance gate and facade are still reminders of glorious days gone by.

A visit at Christmas time will find Freedom Square playing host to the wonderful Christmas market where people keep their hands warm by holding cups of medovina, this is spirit made from honey and served hot. Ideal for keeping the winter chills away!

Spielberg Castle (Hrad Spilberk)

Špilberk 210/1, 662 24 Brno,
Czech Republic
Tel: +420 542 123 611
www.spilberk.cz/

Spielberg Castle is perched high up over Brno and is the most important landmark in the city. Over the centuries it has been the home of the Moravian margraves and a royal castle before becoming a fortress and in later years a brutal prison and then a military barracks.

The castle is also home to the Brno City Museum and within the castle walls there are the small casemates to visit and the lookout tower to climb. The forest and grounds surrounding the castle are popular with local young and old for strolling through, jogging or walking their dogs.

In the museum the exhibitions focus on the role of Spielberg through the years as well as the art and architecture of the city. In the castle visitors can walk through the dark and crowded rooms where some of the toughest and most dangerous criminals of the time were kept.

The opening hours are 9am to 5pm Tuesday to Sunday in May and June and 10am to 6pm Tuesday to Sunday from July to September. In April and October the castle is open from Wednesday to Sunday from 10am to 5pm.

A combined entry ticket for the castle, museum, casemates and tower is CZK250 for adults and CZK150 for concessions. Tickets are also available for each separate part.

Brno Zoo

U zoologické zahrady 147/46
635 00 Brno
Czech Republic
Tel: +420 546 432 311
www.zoobrno.cz/

Brno Zoo is on the outskirts of the city and sprawls across 65 hectares on the forested slopes of Mount Monk. Opened in 1953 the zoo has nearly 1500 animals covering 341 species from the American Bison to the Pig-nosed Turtle. The zoo has a whole range of animals including mammals, birds, reptiles, fish and amphibians.

There are of course zoo favourites such as chimpanzees, seals, sea lions and crocodiles to entertain the crowds while animals from both sides of the Bering Strait can be watched in the Berengia area where the polar bears and Canadian wolves live.

The zoo is home to the threatened Sumatran tiger as well as leopards from Sri Lanka and these beautiful creatures can be observed from specially constructed caves.

The U Tygra restaurant is open all year around and in the summer season there are various refreshment kiosks as well scattered throughout the zoo. There are extra activities for all the family to enjoy such as the Zoo Train, playgrounds, horse riding and trampolines.

The zoo website is in English and full of really useful information. There is a guide to the animal feeding schedule that varies daily so you can time your visit to see your favourite animal being fed. It also describes what events are being held each day. A newborn guide lists all the animals that have been born at the zoo and it is very up-to-date.

You can visit Brno Zoo from November to February between 9am and 4pm, March and October from 9am to 5pm and April through to September from 9am to 6pm. An adult ticket is CZK 100, children concessions pay CZK 70.

Roznov pod Radhostem (Mill Valley Open Air Museum)

Palackého 147, 756 61 Rožnov pod Radhoštěm
Czech Republic
(+420) 571 757 111
www.vmp.cz/

The Mill Valley is a Wallachian open-air museum which comprises the Water Mill, the Saw Mill, the Woollen Mill, the Hammer Mill and the Oil Crusher.

These buildings have been here since 1982 and the idea was to try and recreate forgotten arts and crafts as well as a traditional village of how life used to be. This is an open-air museum on a grand scale and is worthy of allocation a whole day to visit. The journey from Brno takes you through some of the stunning Czech countryside.

At the Mill Valley there is a cultural programme all year round where events are inspired by folklore, the old trades and handicrafts. There are four international festivals each year as well as many small ones and the most popular event is the Rožnov Celebrations.

In Timber Town there are many genuine old wooden houses that were transported from a local village and inside the cottages you can see how the Czech folk lived many years ago. You can walk through the Mayor's Houses, the Post Office, Skittle Alley and Vašek's pub. In St. Anne's Church the beautiful wooden walls are set off by the rather amazing blue-panelled ceiling which is reflected in the highly polished surfaces.

Mill Valley is open at different times according to the time of year and all the details are on the website. The admission prices are also on there as several different ticket combinations are available.

Cathedral of St. Peter & Paul

Petrov 9
602 00 Brno
Czech Republic
Tel: +420 543 235 031
www.katedrala-petrov.cz/

The narrow twin spires of the Cathedral of St. Peter and Paul can be seen from miles around. The cathedral is located on the Petrov hill in the centre of the city and with the spires reaching an impressive 275 feet in the air it is easy to spot.

The two rather intricate towers were built in 1904-1905 by the famous Viennese architect Augustus Kirstein. With its mostly Baroque style interior the cathedral is a very important part of the architecture in South Moravia as well as being a cultural and national monument.

The bells are rung at 11am instead of the more usual noon. During the Thirty Years' War the clever townsfolk repelled the Swedish invasion by ringing the bells an hour earlier. The Swedes had said if they hadn't conquered the town by noon they would leave empty handed. By ringing the bells at 11am the Swedes were fooled and Brno was the only city not to be captured during the war.

The interior of the cathedral is beautiful but it is important not to miss the view from the top of the towers and also go underground to the Romanesque Gothic crypt.

There is a statue of the Madonna and child from around the 14th century, Baroque altars and a late Gothic pieta to admire in the cathedral with its vaulted roof and stained glass windows.

The opening hours are 8.15am to 6.30pm Monday to Saturday and 7am to 6.30pm on Sundays. You can wander round the cathedral independently or guided tours are available.

Villa Tugendhat

Černopolní 45
613 00 Brno
Czech Republic
Tel: +420 515 511 015
www.tugendhat-villa.cz/

This is the beautifully restored and extremely interesting home of Greta and Fitz Tugendhat who lived there in the late 1920's. It was designed by the architect Ludwig Mies van der Rohe and is a shining example of a modern house that was way ahead of its time. It is on the UNESCO World Heritage List and is the only example of modern architecture in the Czech Republic on the UNESCO list.

The house is pretty amazing and you can walk through the various rooms and basements that housed the intricate heating and cooling systems, se the retractable window opening system and the moth-proof room where the precious furs would have been stored. The interior is equipped with identical replicas of the original fixtures and fittings and soft furnishings.

Throughout the summer months various events take place in the pretty and peaceful gardens including films, lectures and concerts.

Villa Tugendhat is open Tuesday to Sunday from 10am to 6pm and tickets can be bought in advance through the website. This is recommended as it does get very, very busy. A basic ticket is CZK300 in the summer but there are concessions.

Capuchin Crypt & Church

Kapucínské nám. 303/5
602 00 Brno
Czech Republic
Tel: +420 511 145 796
www.kapucini.cz/

The pretty pink façade of the Capuchin Church in Brno doesn't give any clues as the gruesome contents and for anyone that likes a spooky experience a visit to the Capuchin Crypt in Brno is a great way to spend a few hours.

The Baroque building has a stunning ceiling fresco by Josef Stern and in the library the original Rococo inventory is still on display. Once you have navigated the narrow passageways where bodies of dignitaries line the walls you pass a woman who was burned alive before you get to the bodies of the 24 monks.

As you enter the crypt a Czech saying "As you are now, we once were; as we are now, you shall be". The naturally mummified remains of the Capuchin order can be seen dating back to the 18th century.

The Capuchin Crypt in Brno is open mid-February to Mid-December, Tuesdays to Saturdays 9am to noon and 1pm to 4.30 pm. Sunday 11am to 11.45am and 1pm to 4.30pm. From May until September the Crypt is also open Mondays.

Moravian Karst, Caves & Cable Car

Jihomoravský kraj
Czech Republic
Tel: +420 516 428 880
www.moravskykras.net/

There are an incredible 1100 gorges and caverns in the Moravian karst area in Central Europe. Out of all of these there are only a few open to the public but they are well worth visiting. The caves and karst area are about 30 miles or so from Brno but you can catch a train from Brno to Blansko then hop on the local bus. This takes you to Skalní Mlyn which is the main access point to the caves and hiking areas.

Some of the valley is closed to cars but cableways and road trains are available to transport visitors from place to place. For hiking fans the Moravian Karst area is covered in colour-coded trails making it easy to find your way through this beautiful landscape.

If you take a cruise through the Punkva Cave you can see the bottom of the famed Macocha Abyss and in Catherine's Cave there are some beautiful and unique limestone columns. Sloup-Šošůvka Caves consist of underground gorges and corridors while in the Balarka Cave the decorative and colourful stalactites will catch your attention.

The Macocha Abyss can also be viewed from two platforms on the Upper and Lower footbridge. One of the mysteries of the Moldavian karst is the Rudice Sink where the Jedovnický potok river disappears underground only to reappear ten miles away.

The opening times and prices of the caves are varied but all the information is available on the website in English to help you plan your visit.

Brno Labyrinth

Zelný trh 21
658 78 Brno-střed
Czech Republic
Tel: +420 542 212 892
www.ticbrno.cz/

Underneath the vegetable market in Brno is a complicated system of cellars and corridors known as the Brno Labyrinth. Many of the cellars date from the Middle Ages although some do go back to Baroque times.

A major reconstruction in 2009 meant that all the cellars and tunnels were finally connected together and then opened to the public in 2011. The biggest cellar is about 75 feet long with a height of 13 feett while the deepest cellar rests 43 feet under street level.

The cellars would have originally been the home for wine maturing in barrels, for keeping food safe and brewing beers. There are 30 or so cellars so there is plenty of room to explore where the medieval townsfolk kept the supplies. To access the cellars there are 212 steps so it is not recommended for people with mobility problems.

The Labyrinth is open all year round from Tuesday to Sunday 9am to 6pm and the entry fee is CZK 160 and CZK 80 for concessions. The entrance is at No 21 in the market square and there is room to leave pushchairs before you descend underground.

Moravian Art Gallery

Husova 18
662 26 Brno
Czech Republic
Tel: +420 532 169 111
www.moravska-galerie.cz/

The Moravian Art Gallery building was constructed in 1882 to house the applied arts of Moravia and Bohemia. The treasures were in such quantity that the museum was extended just six years later and then completely restored at the beginning of the 21st century.

There are three main buildings: Pražák Palace, the Museum of Applied Arts and the Governor's Palace and then the Jurkovič House and Josef Hoffmann Museum.

In the museum there is a permanent exhibition of art from the Middle Ages to the present day. One of the most famous is the head of medusa by Peter Paul Rubens. There are magnificent collections of furniture, metal ware, glass, ceramics, textiles and porcelain. There are also several temporary exhibitions at any one time and visitors can also see the exhibits through a Microgallery virtual tour. In The Camera there is the only dedicated photography exhibition in the Czech art museums.

The opening hours are Wednesday to Sunday from 10am to 6pm and Thursday 10am to 7pm. Entry is free the first Friday of the month to permanent exhibitions in Pražák Palace, the Museum of Applied Arts and the Governor's Palace. On other days a combination ticket for all three buildings costs CZK200 with various discounts for families and concessions.

Recommendations for the Budget Traveller

Places to Stay

Hostel Jacob

Jakubské Námestí 7
Brno 602 00
Czech Republic
Tel: +420 222 539 539
www.hosteljacob.cz/

Hostel Jacob has been around for quite a few years and the owners know what today's travellers expect from their accommodation. The hostel is right in the heart of the city in the pedestrian zone of Jakubské Square so there is plenty going on nearby and any number of places to eat and drink a few steps away.

There are 37 beds across six rooms: you can choose from an apartment, a double room or book a bed in a dorm and save money. In the dorm each bed has curtains for privacy as well as a lamp for reading your Brno travel guide. There are plenty of shared bathrooms, showers and toilets. The bathrooms are clean and well-ventilated and the beds have super comfortable mattresses.

There is a well-equipped communal kitchen with all the appliances necessary for cooking up some snacks but breakfast is included in your room price to start the day off. Free Wifi is available as well as some wired sockets if you prefer. There is a washing machine and dryer available at a small charge but you can iron for free!

Prices start at CZK 400 for a bed in a dorm room and that includes the excellent breakfast with freshly baked bread and freshly brewed coffee.

Hostel Fléda

Štefánikova 24
602 00 Brno
Czech Republic
Tel: +420 731 651 005
www.hostelfleda.com/

Hostel Fléda is the oldest hostel in the city of Brno but with a recent renovation it offers great modern accommodation at a low-cost where you can meet other backpackers. The building used to be a cabaret venue and the spirit lives on as travelling musicians pass through Brno and stay awhile. The hostel has an organised programme of guided tours, barbeques and concerts and they can also help arrange trips and tours for their guests.

In the basement of the building Club Fléda is a great place to listen to music as well as being the biggest club in the region. There is also Báreček, a small bar and courtyard where hostel guests can enjoy beer or coffee at discounted prices.

There are dorms and private rooms with bunk beds or single beds. Lockers are in every room and all sheets and towels are included in the price. Cot and children's bed can be supplied on request and your pet is welcome to stay as well. Bathrooms are shared but they are all super clean and there is plenty of hot water.

Wifi is free and there is a common room and kitchen, luggage storage and a super courtyard with a balcony to enjoy a glass of wine or Moravian beer on.

A bed in a dorm room costs from as little as CZK 250 per person per night while a double room costs CZK680 per room. Breakfast is not included but there are loads of places to eat nearby.

Palacky Hotel & Hostel

Kolejní 2905/2
612 00 Brno
Czech Republic
Tel: +420 541 142 932
www.hotel-palacky.cz/

The Palacky Hotel and Hostel provides reasonably priced accommodation near to the city centre of Brno. There are excellent connections to the motorway meaning that travel times to places like Prague, Vienna and Budapest are cut to the minimum.

It is also convenient for the exhibitions centre where many trade fairs are held and the MOTO GP.

In the hotel there are 30 double rooms all with private bathroom and the hotel is open all the year round. The hostel is seasonal and only open in July, August and part of September. There are 280 double rooms in the hostel all with bathrooms.

There is meeting room for hire for business clients and the 24 hour reception desk offers safety deposit boxes, luggage storage and a fax service. Parking is free and there is room service available.

Breakfast is taken in the Caffe Bar Piccolo while there is a modern self-service pizzeria serving a variety of foods as well as a cafeteria for students.

A double room in the hotel costs from CZK 1360 and in the hostel a double room is CZK 840. Be warned though, the prices do rise quite a bit if there is a trade fair or the MOTO GP on. The prices do include breakfast.

Hostel Mitte

Panská 11, Brno 602 00
Tel: +420 734 622 340
www.hostelmitte.com/

Hostel Mitte has been awarded Hostel of the Year by the Czech Youth Hostel Association and it is a well-deserved title.

This historic building offers great accommodation for your stay in Brno. It is located in the heart of the city and a short walk from the public transport systems, bars and restaurants.

Cosy, peaceful and romantic the Mitte is stylish as well and there is a choice of single, twin or double rooms with a private shared bathroom. There is also a six bed basic dorm room with shared facilities

The rooms are all individually decorated and called after famous events or famous Moravians and on the ground floor a welcoming café has free Wifi and serves excellent drinks.

A bed for the night in the dorm rooms costs from CZK 550.

Ruta 80

Jugoslávská 274/6
613 00 Brno
Czech Republic
Tel: +420 775 396 382
www.ruta80hostel.com/

This city centre hostel is highly recommended and the staff are really friendly and quite happy to sit and chat with you. There is free parking but if you are using public transport the Jugoslavska tram stop is right outside.

Decorated with an eighties style theme you can choose rooms with names like "La Isla Bonita" or the mixed dorm "McFly" room. There are rooms with dorm beds, or single, double and triple rooms to choose from all with shared bathrooms.

Tea and biscuits is available all day but there is a fully functional kitchen for guests to use as well as a common room to meet other travellers in. There is a pleasant terrace to sit and chat over a beer, or two, and the staff speak several languages between them.

A bed in a mixed dorm costs from CZK300 per person per night but if you are travelling with your own sleeping bag discounted rates apply. There are various on-line, long-term and other deals available and all the information is on the website.

Places to Eat & Drink

Café Podnebi

Údolní 222/5, 602 00 Brno, Czech Republic
Tel: +420 542 211 372
www.podnebi.cz/

In the summer months this is a wonderful place to go as there is a large shady terrace and the café is located right under the Spielberg Castle hill. It is a great place for meeting arty and crafty types and if there is live music or theatre on the place is buzzing and crowded.

The aroma of fresh coffee will lure you in and the relaxed bar staff will eventually bring you the menu. All the normal café type refreshments and foods are on offer but the savoury pancakes and Panini's are particularly good. The Brynza and Bacon pancake is full of a soft, salty Slovakian cheese which with crispy bacon is absolutely great.

There is a separate area for smoking which is almost worth visiting just to see the beautiful Bohemian glass ashtrays!

Café Podnebi opens at 8am for breakfast and stays open until midnight.

Vyhlídka Sound Café Bar

Náměstí Svobody 86/17
602 00 Brno
Czech Republic
Tel: +420 602 739 953
www.vyhlidka-cafe.cz/

For some decent music on you rnight out in Brno look out for the Vyhlidka Café on the roof of the Dum panu z Lipe (House of the Lords of Lipe). It is up on the 7th floor and from the terrace there are spectacular views all across the city.

There is an intimate atmosphere with candles on the tables and at around 8pm the DJ starts with his latest mixes. There are several different parts to the café where you can chose to sit at café style tables with bench seats or at high bar tables with stools.

Once a month there is a huge dance party with foreign artists and some of the top Czech DJs come to entertain the crowds. Other events include fashion shows, jam sessions and club concerts.

The opening hours are Monday to Thursday 10am to 2am, Friday 10am to 4am, Saturday 1pm to 4am and Sunday 1pm to 2am.

Restaurant Varna

Solnicni 3a
Brno-Mesto
Czech Republic
Tel: +420 542 210 747
www.restauracevarna.cz

Varna serves traditional Czech food in clean and unpretentious surroundings. There is a good choice of steaks, hamburgers, chicken dishes, pizzas and pastas all well-cooked and nicely presented. There are delicious sounding daily soups, salads and desserts all freshly prepared on the premises.

The menu isn't in English yet but the friendly waiting staff will help you choose something. If all else fails, point to what someone else has!

They do a Saturday three course menu for about CZK 130 and various menus of the day starting at CZK 85. Monthly offers are usually based on a menu from around the world such as Greece and the details and prices are on the website.

To drink they are one of a handful of Brno restaurants serving the 450K lager from the Svijany brewery and every day there are a selection of cocktails to choose from.

The opening hours are Monday 10am to 11pm, Tuesday, Wednesday and Thursday 10am to midnight, Friday 10am until 1am, Saturday 10am to 1am and Sunday noon to 10pm.

Kupe

Veveří 34
602 00 Brno
Czech Republic
Tel: +420 515 544 362
www.kupeorient.cz/

This is a great find if you prefer non-meat meals. Vegetarian, vegan and gluten-free food is served here all freshly prepared from locally grown produce. There is a good selection on the menu, all in Czech, but the pictures are helpful and some of the staff speak basic English.

The restaurant has a comfortable and relaxed feeling, the music is soothing and the service is slow, but worth the wait. A good idea is to order a few dishes and share, the baba ganoush is great and if you are brave enough to finish the whole dish of muhammara dip you get to choose another dish for free.

Turkish pizzas are great and washed down with some Cerna Hora beer are a great way to fill up. The food has a chilli rating for heat but watch out, their assessments are not always accurate!

A light meal for two with a couple of starters and a couple of drinks each will cost about CZK300. Lunchtimes do get busy as they have a special meal deal offer between 11am and 2pm. The website is good and lists the daily specials, although it is all in Czech.

Opening hours are Tuesday to Saturday from 11am to 10pm and Sunday from noon until 10pm.

Pivovarska Starobrno Brewery

Restaurant

Mendlovo náměstí č. 20, Brno 603 00
Czech Republic
Tel.: +420 543 420 130
www.pivovarskabrno.cz/

The brewery has been in Brno in one form or another since 1325 and this is your chance to sample many of the beers from traditional to exciting and special flavours.

Traditional Brno beer is called Starobrno and where better to sample it than at the restaurant attached to the brewery. The main restaurant area is huge and cavernous and the beer hall smoky and noisy but in the summer grab a table on the terrace and enjoy the atmosphere.

From March onwards everyone gathers here round the picnic benches to share the vast quantities of Czech food like pork knuckle with horseradish, mustard and dark Czech bread or goulash stewed with beer.

There is a play area to keep the children occupied and the locals often have their dogs with them. Some of the staff have a few English words and on occasions there is live music and other events happening.

Starobrno is open every day from 10am to midnight.

Places to Shop

Olympia Brno

U dálnice 777, 664 42 Brno-Modřice
Czech Republic
Tel: +420 235 013 437
www.olympia-centrum.com/

Nearly everywhere today has its giant shopping and entertainment complex and Brno is no exception.

Olympia Brno is ideally placed on the southern edge of the city right by the D2 motorway which means access is fast and easy.

There are hundreds of shops, services and specialised outlets to browse round before heading off to the eating area where you can choose between restaurants serving fast food or more traditional meals. There is a cinema and a bowling centre and finally the Albert Hypermarket for all your grocery shopping

All the famous high street brands and designer names can be found under the one roof as well as hairdressers, banks, a post office, a bureau de change, key cutting and a gift wrapping service. There are perfume shops, electronic stores, sports shops, shoes, household, furniture and jewellers all competing for your money.

Children can play at Bamboule or in the Children's Corner and there are specialist children's clothes shops. Outside Olympia Park has the largest outdoor climbing wall in the Czech Republic, an in-line skating track and a miniature train and railway buildings. There are interactive playgrounds, a labyrinth to chase round and water cannons to get your friends and family solaking wet!

At Olympia Brno the shops open from 10am to 9pm weekdays and 9am to 9pm on Saturday and Sunday. The centre itself and the supermarket open earlier than the shops. All details are on the website.

Luta

Veselá
602 00 Brno
Czech Republic
Tel.: +420 542 215 796

This is one of the best known shops for finding traditional Czech gifts and souvenirs. There are dolls dressed in typical Moravian outfits, pottery, hand-painted ceramics, wooden and leather gifts.

Many of the ideas are simple and original

Cabbage Market (Zelny trh)

Namesti Svobody
Brno
Czech Republic

Despite the name it is possible to buy more than just cabbages at this 800 year old market in the centre of Brno. There are fruits and vegetables of all kinds as well as homemade jams and preserves, sweets, flowers and many other items.

The market is a popular place as well for meetings and events even when the market is not on and many photographs are taken showing the central fountain dating from 1690. Like so many other town squares there are several bars and cafés situated around the edge where it is great to sit and enjoy a drink and watch the world pass by.

The opening hours for the market are Monday to Friday from 9am to 6pm and on a Saturday from 9am to noon.

Masarykova Street

Brno
Czech Republic

This wide and pleasant, mainly traffic free street is the heart of shopping in Brno. Just watch out for the number four tram which passes through! Masarykova Street has been used for trading since the 14th century and is one of the oldest streets in the city; it takes its name from the first president of Czechoslovakia.

At street level there are all the shops you could possibly need to browse round from health foods, to sports, to toys and jewellery. Remember to look higher up though as some of the buildings are incredibly ornate and have such history attached to them.

Look out for the beautiful and intricately cut Bohemian crystal and superb glass as well as glittering jewellery featuring the deep red garnets found in the Czech Republic. There are also many art galleries featuring local artists where some superb works can be found.

If you get stuck for somewhere to buy an adaptor or similar hardware items the Cimrman shop has a great selection of stuff.

Bohemia Crystal

Česká 28b
60200 Brno
Czech Republic
Tel. +420 545 566 706
www.crystalporcelan.cz/

A trip to Brno would not be complete without visiting this shop with its dazzling display of Bohemian glass, ceramics and jewellery. You will be spoilt for choice amongst all the glittering gifts. The helpful staff will do their utmost to help you choose the right item.

The Blue Onion china range is vast with everything from gravy boats to plates and storage jars. This is good practical everyday china and is sure to be popular but the Pink Porcelain with its gold trim is exquisitely pretty and would make a lovely gift.

There are plain glasses and delicate crystal glasses which would be ideal with a bottle or two of Moravian wine. The funky Italian Pottery range has chunky cheese knives, pizza plates and spoon rests that would brighten up any gloomy kitchen or dining room. There are gifts by Swarovski and a range of silver jewellery.

The opening times are Monday to Friday from 9am to 6.30pm and Saturday 9am to 12.30pm.

BRNO TRAVEL GUIDE

Printed in Great Britain
by Amazon